Donated by
Peyton
Cunningham
2001   2002

GREAT RECORD BREAKERS IN SPORTS™

TARA LIPINSKI
SUPERSTAR ICE-SKATER

Stasia Ward Kehoe

01-1271

The Rosen Publishing Group's
PowerKids Press™
New York

Published in 2001 by The Rosen Publishing Group, Inc.
29 East 21st Street, New York, NY 10010

First Edition

Book Design: Michael de Guzman

Photo Credits: p. 4 © Shawn Botterill/Allsport; p. 7 © Jamie Squire/Allsport; p. 8 © Todd Warshaw/Allsport, and © Bettmann/CORBIS, and © Robert Landau/CORBIS; p. 11 © J. Barry Mittan; p. 12 © J. Barry Mittan; p. 15 © Otto Creule/Allsport; p. 16 © Doug Pensinger/Allsport; p. 19 © Todd Warshaw/Allsport, and © Aubrey Washington/Allsport; p. 20 © Jamie Squire/Allsport; p. 22 © Todd Warshaw/Allsport.

Kehoe, Stasia Ward, 1968–
    Tara Lipinski, superstar ice-skater / by Stasia Ward Kehoe.
      p. cm.— (Great record breakers in sports)
    Includes index.
    Summary: A biography of the youngest skater ever to win United States and World Figure Skating Championships.
    ISBN 0-8239-5634-2 (lib. bdg. : alk. paper)
    1. Lipinski, Tara, 1982—Juvenile literature. 2. Skaters—United States—Biography—Juvenile literature.
3. Women skaters—United States—Biography—Juvenile literature. [1. Lipinski, Tara, 1982-. 2. Ice skaters.] I. Title.
II. Series.

GV850.L56 K45 2000
796.91′2′092—dc21
[B]
                                              99-059069

Manufactured in the United States of America

CONTENTS

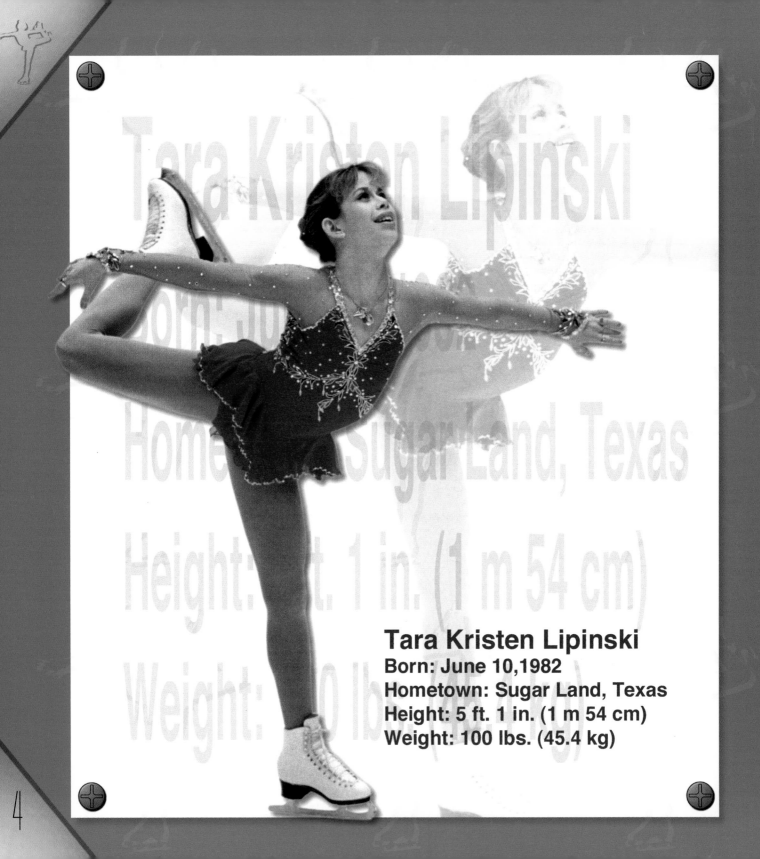

Tara Kristen Lipinski
Born: June 10,1982
Hometown: Sugar Land, Texas
Height: 5 ft. 1 in. (1 m 54 cm)
Weight: 100 lbs. (45.4 kg)

MAKING OLYMPIC HISTORY

The date was February 20, 1998. The place was Nagano, Japan. The event was the women's figure skating **competition** at the **Winter Olympic Games**. Fifteen-year-old American skater Tara Lipinski glided onto the ice. Tara skated beautifully. She landed her jumps perfectly. She finished skating and waited for her scores. Her scores were higher than any other skater's. Tara became the youngest woman skater ever to win an Olympic gold **medal**. A gold medal is an award given to the first-place winner. It was a great day for Tara. She had won many skating awards, but the Olympic gold medal was the greatest prize of all.

◄ *At the Winter Olympic Games, Tara Lipinski skated beautifully for the American team. She was the youngest skater ever to win the gold medal.*

SKATING SCORES

Tara had to win many competitions to reach the Olympics. Ice-skating competitions are made up of a **short program** and a **free skate**. The short program score shows how well the skater did her jumps and other moves. It also shows how hard the program was to perform. The free skate score shows how the judges rank the skater's grace, speed, and style. Judges use a system called OBO, or one-by-one. Each skater's marks, or scores, from each judge are compared to the marks of every other skater. The skater who is ranked highest by the most judges scores a win. In 1998, Tara scored the biggest win of her life.

Tara and her coach, Richard Callaghan, react to Tara's high scores. The area where ice-skaters wait for scores is called the "kiss and cry" area. ▶

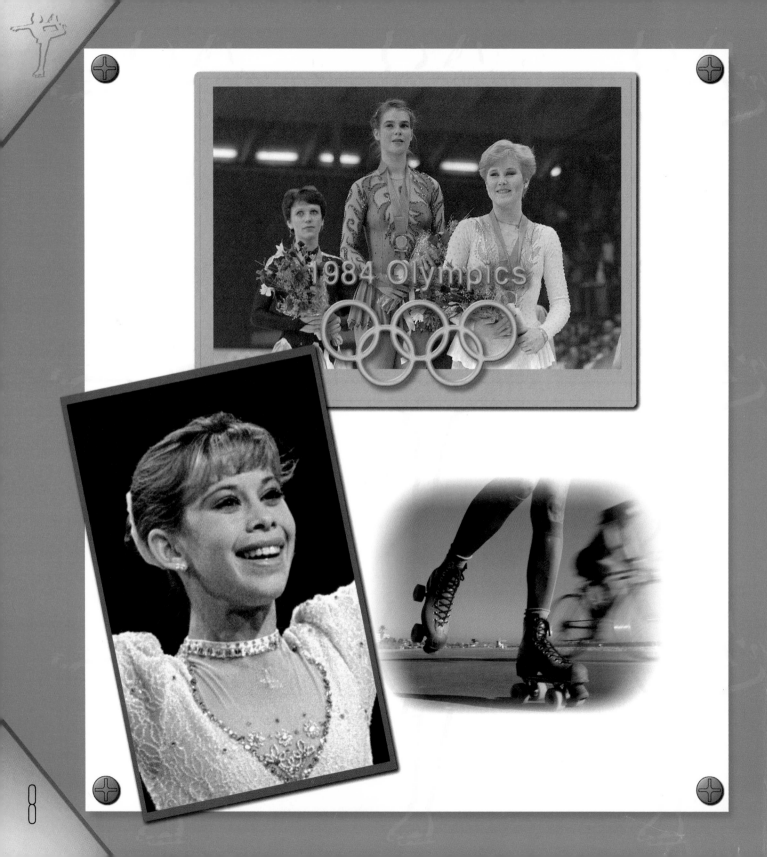

1984 Olympics

A LITTLE GIRL ON WHEELS

Tara Kristen Lipinski was born on June 10, 1982. Her family lived in Sewell, New Jersey. Two-year-old Tara watched the 1984 Olympics on television. She saw the athletes standing on the **podium** to get their medals. Then she stood on an upside-down container and pretended to get a medal of her own. Tara did not know that someday she really would be an Olympic gold **medalist**.

Tara's first sport was roller-skating. She started when she was three years old. She won over 50 trophies, or prizes, for roller-skating. Then Tara's parents took her to an ice rink. Tara loved skating from the first time she stepped onto the ice!

◄ *Tara watched on television as Katarina Witt of East Germany won the gold medal in 1984. Before she became an ice-skater, Tara was a champion roller-skater.*

TIME ON ICE

Six-year-old Tara signed up for lessons at an ice rink in Delaware. It was a one-hour drive from Tara's home in New Jersey. Tara would eat, change into skating clothes, and do her homework in the car while her mom drove to and from the rink. Then Tara's father got a new job. The family moved to Sugar Land, Texas. Tara had to get up at three o'clock in the morning to get time on the nearest ice rink. This **schedule** was very tiring for Tara and her mom.

A coach invited Tara to train with him back in Delaware. The family decided that Tara and her mom should move to Delaware where Tara could have a better practice schedule.

Tara had to practice for five or more hours six days each week to become a great skater. ▶

In 1994, Tara Lipinski became the youngest Olympic Festival gold medalist in any sport.

TARA SETS A RECORD

In the summer of 1994, Tara went to the Olympic Festival in St. Louis, Missouri. Olympic Festivals are not held anymore. The 1994 Olympic Festival was like a practice Olympics. Tara thought the Olympic Festival was very exciting. Her ice-skating was great. The crowd cheered. She won the gold medal. Tara was 12 years and 3 weeks old. This made her the youngest gold medalist in the history of the Olympic Festival. She broke the record held by gymnast Shannon Miller. Shannon had won when she was 12 years and 4 months old. Now Tara was the youngest Olympic Festival gold medalist in any sport!

◀ *Tara skated so well at the 1994 Olympic Festival that the crowd gave her a standing ovation. This means they stood up and clapped loudly.*

A NEW COACH AND A NEW STYLE

After two years in Delaware, Tara and her mom moved to Michigan. Tara wanted to train with Richard Callaghan. He had coached many ice-skating **champions**. Now it was Tara's turn.

Coach Callaghan taught Tara how to practice her jumps in new ways. He worked on getting her to move faster across the ice. He helped her to focus her mind on doing her best. Coach Callaghan thought Tara needed a more **sophisticated** style. Tara chose new, grown-up skating dresses. A famous **choreographer** named Sandra Bezic helped Tara to choose new music. Then Sandra taught Tara great new skating **routines**.

A ballet teacher named Marina Sheffer helped Tara become more graceful on the ice. ▶

Tara Lipinski

TRIPLE TOE LOOP

TRIPLE TOE LOOP–TRIPLE TOE LOOP

Tara's skating routines were getting better and harder. Tara and her coach decided to see if she could land one of the most difficult **combinations** of all. It was a triple toe loop–triple toe loop.

A toe loop is a jump that takes off from the toe pick. The toe pick is a set of ridges on the front of the skate blade. For a triple toe loop an ice-skater has to turn around in the air three times. Tara's combination was two triple toe loops in a row. She practiced hard. At the 1996 United States Postal Service Challenge in Philadelphia, Tara performed the triple toe loop–triple toe loop. She landed it perfectly. She became the first skater to land this combination in competition.

◄ *In 1997, Tara won the United States National Championship. Then at the 1997 World Championships, she was the youngest woman ever to be crowned the world's number-one skater!*

A TOUGH SEASON

The 1997–98 season was not an easy one for Tara. She struggled against sickness. She was not skating as well as she wanted to skate. Instead of first place, she took second place in two important competitions. At the United States National Championships, Tara fell during her short program. She was in fourth place. She needed to move up to win a spot on the Olympic team. She focused on doing her best for the free skate. She landed all of her jumps. Tara moved up to win the silver medal, or second place, and a spot on the 1998 United States Olympic team.

Even good skaters have bad days. In October 1997, Tara fell during her short program at the United States National Championships. ▶

At the age of 15, Tara Lipinski became the youngest ice-skater to win the Olympic gold medal.

GOLD AT NAGANO

The 1998 Winter Olympics were held in Nagano, Japan. The United States sent three women ice-skaters. These ice-skaters were Tara, Nicole Bobek, and Michelle Kwan. Everyone thought Michelle would win the gold. Her ice-skating was very graceful. Tara was a great jumper but people did not think she could be as graceful as Michelle. Michelle skated before Tara. Her moves were beautiful, and her scores seemed unbeatable. Then it was Tara's turn. She skated her best. She had great jumps and was graceful, too. Tara's scores were even higher than Michelle's. At age 15, Tara became the youngest ice-skater to win the Olympic gold medal!

◀ *Winning the gold medal at the 1998 Winter Olympic Games is something Tara will never forget.*

TARA TURNS PRO

Tara had won the Olympic gold medal. What was she going to do next? She thought hard. She decided to become a **professional**, or pro, ice-skater. She joined *Stars on Ice*. Now she travels across America performing with other great ice-skaters such as Scott Hamilton and Kristi Yamaguchi. Fans love to see Tara perform.

Although Tara is a sports record breaker, she has many other talents, too. She is testing her acting skills on television shows like *The Young and the Restless* and *Sabrina the Teenage Witch*. She also acted in a television movie, *Ice Angel*. She works hard and does not give up easily. Champion ice-skater Tara Lipinski is sure to become a record-breaking star off the ice, too.

GLOSSARY

champions (CHAM-pee-unz) People who are the best, or the winners.

choreographer (kor-ee-AH-gruh-fer) A person who makes up dance or sports routines.

combinations (kom-bih-NAY-shunz) Sets of several jumps performed one right after the other.

competition (kom-pih-TIH-shin) A contest to see who is the best at something.

free skate (FREE SKAYT) Also called the long program, it is part of an ice-skating competition, and is usually four minutes for women.

medal (MEH-dul) An award for doing something well.

medalist (MEH-dul-ist) A person who wins a medal.

podium (POH-dee-um) A raised stage.

professional (pro-FEH-shuh-nul) In sports, an athlete who earns money to take part in or play a certain sport.

routines (roo-TEENZ) Worked-out parts, as in dance routines, that may often be done in the same way every time they are performed.

schedule (SKEH-jool) A plan of what one has to do at certain times.

short program (SHORT PRO-gram) Part of an ice-skating competition lasting two minutes and forty seconds.

sophisticated (suh-FIH-stih-kay-ted) Something that is not simple.

Winter Olympic Games (WIN-ter oh-LIHM-pik GAYMS) When the best athletes in the world meet every four years to compete against each other.

INDEX

WEB SITES

To learn more about Tara Lipinski, check out these Web sites:

http://www.taralipinski.com
http://frog.simplenet.com/skateweb/faq/rules.shtml